W9-CFC-193

THE LITTLE BOOK OF
HEXES
FOR WOMEN

The Little Book of

HEXES

For Women

Sophia

**Andrews McMeel
Publishing**

Kansas City

The Little Book of Hexes for Women copyright © 1997 by Sophia. All rights reserved. Printed in the United States of America. No part of this book may be used or reproduced in any manner whatsoever without written permission except in the case of reprints in the context of reviews. For information, write Andrews McMeel Publishing, an Andrews McMeel Universal company, 4520 Main Street, Kansas City, Missouri 64111.

www.andrewsmcmeel.com

The Little Book of Hexes for Women is produced by becker&mayer!, Ltd.

ISBN: 0-8362-3260-7

Edited by Alison Herschberg

Library of Congress Catalog Card Number: 97-71620

00 01 RDC 10 9 8 7 6 5 4

ATTENTION: SCHOOLS AND BUSINESSES

Andrews McMeel books are available at quantity discounts with bulk purchase
for educational, business, or sales promotional use. For information, please write to:
Special Sales Department, Andrews McMeel Publishing, 4520 Main Street, Kansas City,
Missouri 64111.

This book is dedicated to my loving, wonderful husband, Pan.

Introduction

Welcome to the wonderful world of hexes, where you can have the last laugh, where what comes around goes around, and where paybacks are a—well, you get the idea. Is this book for real? Would an intelligent, beautiful, modern woman (that's you, dear) actually cast hexes on people? Of course not! This book is just for fun, a laugh, a harmless way to blow off steam . . . or is it?

Within these pages, you will find all those creeps, geeks, jerks, and snake-dogs (mostly of the male persuasion) who have made your life less than perfect. For every problem you encounter—a nasty landlord, a groping boss, a rude coworker—there are witchy solutions. As you cast these hexes, keep in mind the law of magic:

Once given, three times returned.
Think of this little book as an instant karma-adjustment—
how-to book. Or maybe it's just a little therapy in 112 pages.
Whichever way you choose to put this book to use, just
remember: All power lies within you; never sell yourself
short. I make no claims for the supernatural effectiveness
of these spells—they are strictly for laughs . . . but at whose
expense? Ha ha! To all the nasty little people out there who
are just plain mean, pleasant dreams! And to you, my wild
women readers, happy hexing!

—Sophia

Hex to Humble Techno Snobs

Do we average mortals really need to know about multilevel interfaces, programming language, or hypertext markup whatever? It's enough just to turn on those digital monsters! Techno snobs who think you are ignorant and worthless because of your lack of techno knowledge need to be knocked down a notch. This hex will remind those Vulcan techno nerds that it's not nice to be pompous—even in the '90s!

You Will Need

+ a small floppy disk
+ a red pen
+ an envelope
+ a stamp

The Spell

First write a letter on your computer and save it onto the disk. In the letter, write everything you've ever wanted to say to the idiot in question, about: his rudeness, condescending attitude, etc. When you have saved the letter, eject the disk. On the label, clearly write, "Never Damage!!!"

Then break it, smash it, stomp it, soak it, etc., saying:

The hurts you gave
Go back to you.
Think this clearly
Think it through.
The mind is not all,
From hubris you'll fall!
Slip off your throne,

To me you'll atone!
Colagula et solve!

After you've recited this chant, throw the broken disk into the envelope and send it to the person or leave it for him on his desk. Include a small note which should read something like this:

"This disk contains extremely important information. You, of all people, should be able to get the information off of it, right? Thanks a bunch!
Yrs, (something completely illegible)"

When the know-it-all encounters the disk, he will get more and more confused. The next time you see him, he should be much more humble.

For People Who Always Tell the Ends of Movies or Books

Sounds like a great movie, right? Or maybe the newest, hottest video has just landed in your hands— something to look forward to. Then The Spoiler appears. You know, that person who always tells you the ending: "Oops! Sorry!" Well, this little spell will knock that off fast!

You Will Need

+ a small piece of yarn or thread, preferably from the person in question, but any will do in a pinch

THE SPELL

Look at that person (or at least intently think of his or
her face), take the cord, and, at the dark of the moon,
knot it three times, saying:

Ending's ending
Soon will be
By the tying
Of tongue by three.
Silent you shall be
To me,
By my silence
May it be!

Then put a finger to your lips and be completely silent for
one minute, visualizing the person in question as likewise
silent. Leave the knotted cord somewhere where the
person will be, or bury it deep in the ground.

A Spell for People Who Always One-Up You

You're steaming, flames spouting from your ears. That person just made you look like a fool . . . again. Here is how to shatter that smug, one-up veneer and tip the balance.

You Will Need
+ a dollar bill—the rattiest, dirtiest dollar you can find
(Try to get it from a real lowlife at a truly
nasty business establishment.)
+ a match

The Spell
At midnight, light a small corner of the dollar bill on fire,
say the person's name three times, then say:

You think you are green,
You think you are gold,
You think you are hot,
And will never grow old!

Blow out the corner of the burning bill, crush it in your fist,
toss it to the ground, then step on it, saying:

Now here you go.
Now under my toe!
So much for your snub—
Now here's the rub!

After you've recited the hex, pick up the bill from the
ground. Later, drop it near the person and say, "Oh, you
dropped this!" Pick it up and hand it to them with a
knowing smile, and watch the cookie crumble!

A Spell to Turn Aside True Believers

If someone you know has a Cause and insists upon hitting
you over the head with it every chance they get, this
little charm will cause them to corner someone
else at the snack bar.

You Will Need
+ some lavender or lavender oil

The Spell
Place the lavender in your pocket
(or put some oil on) and say:

BLOW AWAY,
FLOW AWAY,
PASSION'S WORDS
WILL NOT STAY.
MY TRUE HEART
YOU CAN NOT SWAY,
LET YOUR BABBLE
FADE AWAY!

Wave the scent around your body counterclockwise.
See it form a light purple haze about you which deflects
all bull. When you meet the True Believer and he begins
his rap about the Cause, interrupt him and say, "Smell this,
isn't it lovely?" and let him sniff the lavender. Before he
resumes the lecture, say, "See you!" and vanish.
That'll do it.

A Spell to Muffle Diet Queens

She's your friend, but you just can't listen any more when she starts talking about her 718th diet. All the trials and tribulations that go with losing weight—*who cares!?* Lose weight already or hush! Back up that feeling with this one.

You Will Need
+ a piece of her worst diet enemy; if it's chocolate, get a whole candy bar
+ a black pen

The Spell
Take the chocolate bar and draw a circle with a line through it on the wrapper. Then say:

Do it truly or get hence,
Keep your struggle
In silence!
Accept yourself
As you are,
If you do you will go far!
Felicitas!

The next time you see her, give her the candy bar and make her chow down. Henceforth, the diet struggle should either cease or remain blissfully unknown to others.

SPELL TO SILENCE WHISTLERS AND HUMMERS

Lalalalala, mmm mm mmmm mm mmm, tweet tweeeet tweet . . . If you were living in a pet store or yoga school, it might not bother you. But there is such a thing as noise pollution, and sometimes it has two legs. Why does this person hum or whistle around you all the time? Pull the plug!

THE SPELL

Next time the situation arises, depending on what the offender is doing, hum or whistle quietly into the four directions, down, and up. Then whisper:

ECHO STEALS ECHO
SOUND CANCELS SOUND.
WHAT VIBRATES TO ME
NOW GOES AROUND!

Then clap your hands and say:

AROUND AND ABOUT,
ALL NOISE IS OUT!

Hear the sounds of the noisy one fade like a passing wind.
Ahhh . . . silence!

Spell to Stop Those Catcalls Cold

You look good—you always do. But that's no reason for
lowlife scum to whistle at you while making rude and
uncivilized gestures. Usually you just ignore them and
steam, but no longer. Send it back at them! Zap!

You Will Need
◆ You don't need anything special for this spell,
just a righteous attitude.

The Spell
When you hear the idiots begin their adolescent posturing,
ignore them . . . for a while. When you've had enough, feel
your anger grow cold and electric. When your energy is
really up, turn and look at the culprits.

Make the sign of the fig with your right hand, thumb thrust
through your fingers when making a fist. Close your left eye
and beam at them with your right eye. Blast them with
all your energy, whispering:

MALO! MALO! MALO!

Then spit on the ground and walk away. Silence!

A Spell to Discourage Copycats

You did it first, they got the credit. You told that story,
now the copycat is telling it! It's as true today as it was in
first grade—copycats are a pain! This spell will keep
your uniqueness intact. Works especially well in an
office situation.

You Will Need
+ three wastebaskets
+ a copy machine

The Spell
Place the wastebaskets in a wide circle around the copycat's
desk. Get your hands on an image or signature of the
copycat. Go to the Xerox machine and make three
copies while saying:

Copy, copy
You can see.
What you copy
Comes from me.
You must halt
You mustn't do!
What I do;
You are through!
Janus!

After reciting these words, carefully toss each of the
copies in the wastebaskets while saying:

It is over
You are done.
Go elsewhere to have your fun.
You no longer fix on me,
As i will so may it be!

Unique you will stay!

To Halt People without Privacy Borders

How's your lover? How much did that cost? Who ya talking to? Where are you going tonight? Yak, yak, pry, pry. It's amazing how intrusive some people can be. This little number will enforce your personal boundaries.

You Will Need
+ salt
+ a small letter opener

The Spell
When no one is around, go to the place you normally get harassed. Sprinkle salt around you three times, saying:

Off of me, out of me, away from me,

LET ME BE, LET ME BE, LET ME BE!
MY LIFE IS MY OWN,
YOU I DISOWN,
PESTER ME NOT,
OR YOU WILL ROT!

Now take out the letter opener and hold it
straight up, saying:

I AM SHIELDED,
I'M SEALED TIGHT,
I'M PROTECTED,
BY SWORD'S MIGHT!

Visualize a silver globe protecting you from the nosy one,
then place the letter opener somewhere nearby. Later,
when the nosy one starts poking for details, pick up the
letter opener and begin to play with it. Visualize the silver
globe and smile—soon he or she will be gone!

Hex for People Who Eat Your Food

Everyone knows them—the tasters, biters, and nibblers:
"Can I have just an itty-bitty taste? You don't mind if I
nibble, do you?" Suddenly that lovely meal you were all set
to enjoy is marred by The Mooch again. Yuck!
Here's how to put a stop to it.

You Will Need
+ a table knife
+ some pepper

The Spell
When The Mooch approaches, be ready. Have the knife set
on the table in front of your plate, away from you. Have the
pepper ready. When he moves in for the munch, glance at

the person, sprinkling pepper on and about
your food, whispering:

> PEPPER FLY AND FLY AWAY,
> NO FOOD FOR YOU, GO AWAY!

When The Mooch begins to drool and slide toward your
food, pick up the knife, making sure he sees it, then drop it
as if by accident, saying something like, "My goodness, I'm
not safe to be around when I'm eating!" Then smile.

When he leaves, blow some pepper at his back, saying:

> PEPPER FLY AND FLY AWAY,
> NO FOOD FOR YOU, GO AWAY!
> MY FOOD IS MINE, SO IT SHALL STAY!

Now enjoy your meal in peace.

Hex for People Who Talk during Movies

For some of us, cinema is sacred. What possesses some people to become flaming loudmouths in a movie theater? Do we really need more inane comments in this world? I think not. Try this one and do your part to halt this horror.

You Will Need
+ a piece of black cord

The Spell
The next time you go to a movie, be prepared. When some fool starts jabbering during the film, get out your cord and tie the ends together, whispering:

OPEN MOUTH,
EMPTY HEAD.

Then tie a knot in the middle of the whole thing, saying:

CLOSE IT NOW,
LISTEN INSTEAD!

After you've recited these words, laugh at an inappropriate
time and glance at her. Leave the cord under the loudmouth's chair when you leave the theater.

Hex to Stop that Chump from Calling

You cringe when you hear who is on the phone for you.
Again? Some people just don't think before they dial those
numbers—but this hex is a real communicator!

You Will Need
+ a red pencil

The Spell
When you've got the irritating one on the phone,
take your red pencil and lightly draw this pattern
over the earpiece grid.

Hold the phone away from you as he babbles on,
and whisper:

Like a beam,
Like a ray,
Pass on through,
Go away!
Gone tomorrow,
Gone today!

Then suddenly excuse yourself due to some strange
emergency and slam the phone down saying:

Hut kut!
You are out,
You are gone,
There's no doubt,
Sut!

That ought to do it.

A Hex for People Who Impose on Your Clothes

Remember where that favorite sweater is? Oh, yes, so-and-so borrowed it, "Just for a bit," ages ago. Or maybe you did get it back . . . with some extra decorations. Shame! Clothes vandals are the worst kind. Here's how to rinse their load!

You Will Need
+ some article he or she borrowed
+ something with thorns (A rose stem or some blackberry vine will do.)

The Spell
Visualize the borrower. Get stomping mad and swing the article of clothing around over your head and say:

YOU, YOU ABUSED.
FEEL HOW I FEEL.
YOU, YOU MISUSED,
THIS DAMAGE IS REAL.
YOU, YOU ARE REFUSED,
NOW IT IS SEALED!

Wrap the clothing around the thorns (try not to snag it) and
stomp on the ground three times, saying:

BACK AT YOU,
FEEL WHAT I DO,
THINK ABOUT ANOTHER,
NO ONE YOU BOTHER.
YA!

Wash the garment immediately or toss it.
It won't happen again!

A Hex on Phone and Door-to-Door Solicitors

Is it just me, or have charities, siding companies, and credit card companies multiplied beyond human comprehension? At least half of the calls and unexpected knocks at the door seem to be solicitors. We only have so much to give! Stop the madness! This is an old one.

You Will Need
+ lots of pennies
+ a knife

The Spell
At the dark of the moon, go outside and scratch an X into as many pennies as you'll need for the coming month. As you do so, say:

I AM CROSS AND YOU ARE CROSSED.
YOU'VE BOTHERED ME SO YOU'LL BE TOSSED!
KEEP YOUR WHINING, HALT YOUR CRIES, HECATE!
AS THE CROSSED COIN FLIES!

Toss the pennies lightly in the air and see all the junk mail, calls, etc. fly away from you. Then go to sleep. When you wake the next day, pick up the pennies and keep them somewhere safe. The next time you get a junk-mail plea, send them a penny. When someone knocks on your door, give him or her a penny. If someone calls you on the phone, tap the coin on the receiver while getting rid of him or her, then toss it into some bushes. Each time you use a coin, say:

CROSSED AND OUT,
DOWN AND ABOUT,
HIGH AND LOW,
CROSS COIN GO!

A Hex for People Who Are Always on the Phone (yak . . . yak . . . yak . . .)

These people can tie up a phone line for hours, talking about . . . nothing! It is remarkable, but it can go beyond irritating. When enough is enough, pull the plug with this little number!

You Will Need
+ a black feather
+ patchouli oil

THE SPELL

At night, when the moon is half-waning, dip the black
feather in the oil and draw a W in the air over the
telephone in question or in the direction of the culprit
who is calling you, saying:

CHATTER, CHATTER, EMPTY MATTER,
BLOW AWAY, THROW AWAY.
CEASE BY NIGHT, CEASE BY DAY!
SATURNUS VERUM!

Place the feather under the phone and picture the
person in question avoiding the phone altogether.
Put your finger to your lips, then leave.

A Gentle Little Hex to Calm Down "Type-A" People

Hyper-tense, histrionic, energetic, irrepressible, and wound tighter than a watch—don't we just love these types of people? Let's face it, without them we'd all still be huddled around campfires in skins, but they can still grate on our nerves. When that "Type-A" person is going over the top, this will bring the energy level down a bit.

You Will Need

+ a small piece of paper
+ an orange pen or pencil

The Spell

Write this charm on the piece of paper using your orange writing utensil. Speak each word as you write it:

Agenona
Agenon
Ageno
Agen
Age
Ag
A

Then say:

(name) is calm
(name) is free
Of stress tension
And misery.
As I will,
So it shall be!

Place the paper under the hyper person's seat. Voilà!

A Hex for Halting Garden Thieves

Do you dirty your hands, bend your back, and muck around
in your garden just so someone (or something) can come
along and steal from or damage it? I don't think so. Help is
at hand with this little "green thumb" hex.

You Will Need

+ a small forked branch in the shape of a Y
+ water
+ vinegar

The Spell

Take the branch and clean it. Mix the water and vinegar
together. At dawn or sometime in the morning, hold the
branch while sprinkling the vinegar and water
mixture about the garden, saying:

TREAD NOT HERE,
TREAD NOT THERE,
TOUCH NO PLANT,
ALL BEWARE!
ELHAZ!

When you are done, stick the branch into the ground in the center of the garden, somewhat hidden, saying:

YOU ARE BANISHED BY THE THREE,
COME TOO CLOSE AND YOU MUST FLEE,
BY THIS MARK SO SHALL IT BE!

See how they run!

Touchy-Feely Hex to Keep Away Space-Invading People

You are as affectionate as the next person, but there are such things as personal borders. Do you really want to *kissy-kissy* or *big bear hug* anyone off the street? Ugh! When people get a little too touchy-feely with you, here's a way to tactfully draw the line.

You Will Need
+ a dried red chili pepper
+ a safety pin

The Spell
At midday stand alone in the sun if possible.
Pin the pepper to the inside of your jacket and say:

HOT TO SMELL,
HOT TO TOUCH,
BE NICE TO ME,
BUT NOT TOO MUCH!
HUG ME HARD AND YOU WILL BURN,
KISS ME AND YOUR FACE WILL TURN!

Turn around clockwise three times and
stamp your feet three times. Then say:

THIS IS MY SPACE,
KEEP YOUR PLACE!

This works better (and longer) than pepper spray!
Watch her face the next time she tries to smooch!
Bury the pepper when you are done with it.

HEX FOR CUTESY-WOOTSIE COUPLES

Honey sweetie pie! Darling snookums cuddle bunny boo boo! Kissy love muffin! Sugar candy baby bunky! Yuck! Enough already! Sure love makes the world go 'round, but saccharine, cheesy pet names only turn the stomach! When you've been assaulted with enough sugar-coated love babble, fight back!

You Will Need
+ sugar
+ a broom

The Spell
Take the sugar and scatter it in a spiral around where the lovebirds will flutter, saying:

WORDS OF SUGAR,
MELT AWAY!
SAVE IT FOR
ANOTHER DAY!

Then, after they are gone, sweep the sugar out the
door after them, saying:

KAMA!
SHOW YOUR REAL LOVE
WITH TRUTH AND AFFECTION.
I BRUSH YOUR WORDS
IN ANOTHER DIRECTION!

The next time you see the sweetie pies, they'll either
be necking or civil-tongued!

A Hex for People Who
Leave You Waiting

It's been an hour and you're fuming. That lame fool has
stood you up! Okay, maybe there is a good reason—but not
only was your time wasted, the rest of the afternoon or
evening was pretty much spoiled too! Don't wallow in bad
feelings, dump them back in the no-show's lap!

You Will Need
+ an alarm clock with a particularly obnoxious alarm
+ a telephone

The Spell
Hold the clock to the four directions, saying each time:

TIME AND TIDE WON'T WAIT FOR YOU.
TIDE AND TIME NOW MAKE THIS TRUE!
YOU LEFT ME AND NOW I SAY,
WHAT YOU HAD WILL FLY AWAY!
TEMPUS FUGIT!

Now set the alarm and call that worthless no-show. When you get the answering machine or the person you're after, set off the alarm. Count to ten and hang up (unless he or she hangs up first).

Before you turn off the alarm, whisper the above verse one last time. Expect an apology; demand a lot more than that.

To Return Bad Energy from a Hateful Letter or Document

Poison pen letters, nasty memos, and snide notes are
sometimes the most awful things to receive. Here is a
spell to wash them off you and toss the mess
back from whence it came.

You Will Need
+ a red pen
+ an envelope
+ matches
+ a black feather
+ a stamp

THE SPELL

Using the red pen, address the envelope to the offending
party. Do not use a return address. Take the offending
letter or document and burn it, making sure to save
the ashes, and recite this chant:

ANGER AND INSULT BACK TO YOU.
AS YOU ACT, SO SHALL YOU DO.
JUSTICE, BALANCE, HONOR, AND RIGHT,
I FLING IT BACK WITH ALL MY MIGHT!
AVERT! AVERT!

Crumble the ashes into the envelope, add the feather,
and send it to the offending party.

The Unruly Neighbor Spell

Do you have a neighbor who is driving you crazy? Have you
talked to her and tried to resolve disputes, only to have her
spread ugly rumors about you and your loved ones?
If you want her pettiness to go back to her,
try this spell.

You Will Need
+ one small mirror

The Spell
At noon, take a small mirror and prop it up so it faces the
direction of your neighbor's home, reflecting toward her.
Then say these words:

WHATEVER YOU SAY ABOUT ME,
NOW REFLECTS BACK TO THEE.
AVERT! AVERT! AVERT! BACK TO THEE!

Say this spell three times, then spit in the direction of
the neighbor. Leave the mirror there for one full month.
Repeat as necessary.

To Discourage an Unwelcome Suitor

It's simple. He likes you, maybe even loves you! You couldn't care less. You're a goddess. It happens. Send the poor fool gently away with this spell.

You Will Need
+ something the suitor has given you
+ a purple pen
+ matches

The Spell
On something the suitor has given you,
write the following in purple ink:

Fascination
Fascinatio
Fascinati

FASCINAT
FASCINA
FASCIN
FASCI
FASC
FAS
FA
F

Then say each word, ending the chant with these words:

REDUCE, DIMINISH!
AFTER THAT, FINISH!
WE CAN NEVER BE,
I SET YOU FREE!
GOOD-BYE!

Then burn the scrap. If he bothers you again,
send him the ashes!

Spell to Curse a Liar to Tell the Truth

Those little white lies can reveal black little hearts.
If someone is lying to you or about you in a
malicious manner, balance the scales.

You Will Need
+ a black feather

The Spell
Take the black feather and clean it lightly in water. On a
new moon, hold the feather to the sky and say:

Wings of justice
In sky and sea,
Hear my chant,

COME TO ME.
BRING THE BALANCE,
BRING THE TRUE,
AS THIS FEATHER
TO ME FLEW!
MAATI!

Give the feather to the liar or place it in a
personal space of his or hers, and say:

HERE IS THE BALANCE,
HERE IS THE TRUE.
CONJURED WITH MY HURT,
I BRING IT HERE TO YOU.
DON'T CONCEAL IT.
NOW REVEAL IT!

The truth will come out.

Spell to "Fix" Just Downright Mean People

We have all tangled with mean folks. You know what I mean—the real nasties who seem to exist just to spite people and cause misery. Here is how to dissolve them from your reality.

The Spell

When the mean person approaches you, imagine that you are holding a mirror up so that the mean person sees his own reflection. Concentrate all your energy back into the mirror image, as you say this to yourself:

I AM STRONG,
I AM GOOD!
MEAN PERSON
GET WHAT YOU SHOULD . . .
You!

He will stop in his tracks—even mean people do not like meanness. When I use this spell, the mean person usually forgets what he wanted to spew and goes away.

Spell to Repel Sexual Harassment

Leeches are people who leer, or who talk to your breasts instead of your face. Every woman, with the exception of nuns, perhaps, has dealt with this lower life-form since puberty. Here is how you can deal with leeches.

You Will Need
+ a condom
+ a thorn from a rose
+ a stick of incense

The Spell
While visualizing the aforementioned leech, take the condom and prick it with the thorn.
Light the incense while saying:

YOU HAVE HARASSED ME,
YOUR DAY IS DONE.
NEVER WILL YOU HAVE ANOTHER ONE!

Toss the condom in the trash, where this person belongs.

SPELL FOR PEOPLE WHO STEAL YOUR PARKING SPOT

This happens to all of us. Nothing is worse than driving
around for hours and not being able to find a place to park.
Then, just when you find one, some jerk moves in and
knocks you out of your place. Nothing you can do
about it except cast this spell.

THE SPELL
First cross your fingers, point them at the
evil driver, and say:

CAR TROUBLE, CAR TROUBLE
COMING YOUR WAY!
YOU BLEW ME OFF
AND NOW YOU'VE GOT TO PAY!

Hiss at the driver and go find another spot.
To accomplish this, chant:

GREAT GODDESS SQUAT, FIND ME A PARKING SPOT!

Say this out loud while looking for a spot. This should
do the trick. Offer the great goddess cushion crumbs
when you find a place.

Spell to Spite People Who
Stand You Up

It's happened again, and she even got to choose the time
and place! First find out if your date had a good reason for
her absentia, so you will not suffer any guilt for blasting
her. Then get ready to teach her a lesson.

The Spell
Go to the person's house. Seethe with rage. Point at the
house and envision a lightning bolt in the sky, then chant:

LATE AND ABSENT, SO YOU WILL BE!
SOON ALL YOU CALL WILL SHUN THEE!
TO COVENTRY!

Repeat this chant three times at the top of your voice,
pointing a finger (you know which one) in the direction
of the person's home. Then laugh crazily.

SPELL TO BAN PEOPLE WHO TELL YOU ALL OF THEIR PROBLEMS

Some folks can't wait to strike up a conversation that you are not interested in pursuing. Too often the subject is their personal problems. What do you do?

THE SPELL
When you take out the trash, visualize the person as you toss it, saying:

DUMP IT SOMEWHERE ELSE!
DUMP IT IN THIS CAN!
DUMP IT ON A DOG!

Dump it on a man!
Dump it in the water!
Dump it in the air!
Dump it far away from me
Because i just don't care!

Slam the lid down. The next time you see The Dumper,
smile and breeze past.

Spell for Someone Who Cuts You Off on the Road

This spell takes the fear that is inflicted on you by
someone who cuts you off (without signaling, of course),
and bounces it back to them, causing him or her
to get cut off by someone else.
Paybacks are a bitch.

The Spell

Beep your horn, and make the Sign of the Horns—
you know, thumb and pinky raised. Point the horns
at the offending driver, and send all your adrenaline
energy back at him or her, saying:

ON YOUR HEAD, ON YOUR HEAD,
BECAUSE OF YOU I COULD BE DEAD!
ALL MY FRIGHT TO YOU IS DUE!
IT FLIES FROM ME AND LANDS ON YOU!
YAAAAAAA!

Then honk the horn briefly again to send the spell.

Spell to Banish a Troublesome Coworker or Acquaintance

Doll magic has been around for thousands of years. From voodoo dolls to Chinese paper charm-dolls, using them wisely can reap great benefits. I am not suggesting that you stick pins in your doll and expect your enemy to writhe in pain. This is, after all, a Hollywood version of doll magic (although you might give it a try). This is a good hex to get someone to leave you alone, though! Although your coworker or acquaintance will not disappear, he or she may ignore you—which is all you want. Here is how you do it.

You Will Need
+ a piece of paper
+ scissors
+ a pen
+ a match

The Spell

Cut out a paper doll and write the person's
name on it, all the time saying:

LEAVE ME ALONE!
LEAVE ME IN PEACE!
FIND ANOTHER WAY
TO SPREAD YOUR DISEASE!

Take the doll and burn it, visualizing your enemy going
away. Throw the ashes to the wind.

When Passed Over for a Promotion (for Someone Less Qualified)

Office politics, especially between women, are the worst. You all know what I mean. When you get outsmarted, get even.

You Will Need
+ an envelope
+ something belonging to your rival
+ two playing cards (or copies of cards):
the ace of spades and the five of clubs
+ a stamp
+ a camera
+ a green candle
+ a match

THE SPELL

In the envelope, place the object from your rival with the playing cards. Pick a nasty city and address the envelope to the local post office there, "*To hold for (name) . . .*" Don't use a return address. Make sure to pick the place that your rival would most hate having anything to do with. After you have sent the letter, display a picture of yourself and light a green candle before you go to bed. As you light the candle, visualize the job that you desire the most in this world, and believe that you will get that job.

Burn the candle every night until it is gone, and say:

BLOW AWAY, BURN AWAY.
I GET TOMORROW, YOU LOSE TODAY!

To Repel a Stalker or Unwanted Follower

A spell for creeps who do not take the hint. This spell should be followed up with police action, if necessary.

You Will Need
+ two chicken bones, cleaned
+ some red thread

The Spell
Tie the chicken bones together with the thread in the form of a cross. Formulate a vision of the creep in question, running away in horror. Now chant:

OUT, OUT, AWAY, AWAY!
BY BONE AND BLOOD, DO AS I SAY.
BANISHED, REPELLED, FORGOTTEN, GONE!
YOU ARE BANNED BY THE CROSSING BONE!

After you have recited the chant, spit on the crossed bones
three times and bury them in front of your residence. The
creep should never bother you again.

Spell for Rip-Off Repairmen

If you have been taken advantage of by a repairman
or salesperson just because you are a woman,
this spell should help.

You Will Need
+ herbal incense (bay leaves are very good)
+ a photocopy of the object you bought
or had repaired, or a sales slip
+ envelope
+ stamp
+ dirt

THE SPELL

Light the incense. When the smoke starts to rise, project thoughts of all of the offending person's business dissolving into thin air. Tear the sales slip (if you have it) into shreds and chant:

JUSTICE BE DONE QUICK,
SAVE ME, SAVE ME!
HERM! HERM!

Next write a letter to the offender saying everything you wished you had said to his or her face. Send the letter with the dirt and ashes from the incense.

Spell to Keep Smokers Away

You ask nicely. There are signs everywhere. You try to remain civil, but some people just don't get it. No problem. Try this one.

You Will Need
+ a cigarette

The Spell
Take the cigarette and point in the four directions and up, then chant:

Smoke away, float away,
Banned by night, gone by day!
Burn away from,
Turn away from,
Stay
Far, far, far
Away from me!
So may it be!

Break the cigarette in half, fling the pieces into a garbage
can, and stamp your foot!

To Halt Vicious Gossip

No one knows why people gossip, but when the digs are
at your expense, dearie—fight back!

You Will Need
+ a small mirror
+ a black marker

The Spell
Take the mirror and use the black marker to draw a
heart with an eye in the middle. Draw a tear coming
from the eye, and say:

SEE THE DARKNESS THAT YOU SPREAD,
WITH YOUR HEART AND WITH YOUR HEAD.
STOP YOUR EVIL, HALT YOUR SPITE!
THIS I DEMAND, MAKE IT RIGHT!

Place a real tear on the mirror and leave it where the
offending party will find it. Never tell a soul what you did.

A Bad Haircut Revenge Spell

Ruined your 'do and they won't even knock five
dollars off the tab? Well you can't get your hair back,
but you can do this.

You Will Need
+ a strand of your hair
+ the hairdresser's business card

The Spell
Take the strand of your hair, wrap it around the
business card, and say:

LOCKS OF MINE THAT ARE NOW DEAD,
GROW ME SOME NEW ONES INSTEAD.
MAY THE ONE WHO GAVE ME HAIR TO HATE
HAVE BAD HAIR UNTIL THIS DATE!
(PICK A DAY, MONTH, AND YEAR)

Burn the card and scatter the ashes in the wind.
Your hairdresser's hair will be unmanageable
until the date that you picked.

Spell to Wake Up and Motivate a Couch Potato

That man just lays there like a slug. Shame! This will light a fire under that lazy butt, and he'll end up thanking you!

You Will Need
+ a pen
+ a piece of red paper

The Spell
Draw this figure on the red piece of paper, and say:

Move and go forth!
Here not lie!
Fan the spark of life,
Never let it die!
Up and out on the earth,
Each day is a rebirth!
Motivate and celebrate now!

Repeat as necessary.

Hex for Protection from Sloppy Drunks

We've all had them hang on us, drool on us, rub past us,
and so on. The worst kind of men in their weakest
moments. Is there anything so pathetic as a drunk idiot?
Put him out of his misery, girls.

You Will Need
+ a glass of the drunk's drink of choice

The Spell
If a drunk is bothering you, pour a few drops of beverage
on the floor. Turn away and picture yourself pushing
him away while saying:

AVANT AVERT!
AWAY AND BEGONE,
TURN AWAY; GO!
STAY NOT LONG!
SPIRITS OF SPIRITS
PULL, PUSH, AND FLOW.
YOU CAN NOT COME
YOU; NOW; GO!
AVERT!

Hex to Halt Excessive Foul Language

Those #∂%! people who can't keep their #∂%! mouths closed! Aren't you tired of hearing #∂%! every time you have a conversation with them? Maybe this hex will help them see the light.

You Will Need
+ small pieces of scrap paper
+ a pen
+ a piece of the loudmouth's clothing
  or something personal
+ a paper bag
+ some string

THE SPELL

Write the words most commonly used by the loudmouth on small pieces of paper. Take the piece of his clothing, all of the pieces of paper, and put them in a bag. Tie some string around the bag while saying:

SILENCE, QUIET,
KEEP THEM OUT.
NEVER WHISPER, NEVER SHOUT.
BANISH, EDIT, CUT, AND BEND,
ALL THIS CUSSING,
IT MUST END!

Then bury the bag while saying:

DOWN AND DEEP,
LET THEM SLEEP,
AND SO THE AIR IS CLEAR!

Hex to Banish Strangers Who Judge You

Some people's hobby is to judge other people. The next time you feel yourself being judged by a stranger, turn your back to her, and use this spell.

You Will Need
+ a small mirror or piece of mirror

The Spell
Catch his or her reflection in the mirror. Turn your back to the judge, and recite these words:

BEGONE YOU TO ANOTHER PLACE.
DO NOT JUDGE ME,
IT'S NOT YOUR SPACE!

Say this twice and go outside. Visualize the earth swallowing her up as you bury the mirror in some dirt. Walk away.

Hex for Someone Who Is Cruel to Animals

What kinds of people mistreat animals? Sick?
Twisted? Surely they deserve nothing less
than the full hex treatment.
Don't forget a backup call to the ASPCA or PAWS!

You Will Need
+ a stick
+ a paintbrush
+ some red paint

The Spell
Paint three X s in a row on the stick.
As you paint each X , say:

THE PAIN YOU INFLICT
RETURNS NOW TO YOU.
ALL HEAR WHAT YOU SAY,
AND SEE WHAT YOU DO!

Strike the earth three times with the stick, saying:

HEAR ME ALL NATURE,
ALL ANIMALS AND LIFE!
HALT THIS ABUSE,
THIS ANGER AND STRIFE!

Late at night, howl (Awooooooo!) and throw the stick
in front of the abuser's house or driveway.
Make sure that he or she will find it.

A Hex for Bad Landlords

Let's face it—we have enough trials just getting through life without needing to worry about repairs, stopped-up sinks, threatening notes, and the like. Get that landlord back into line with this one.

You Will Need
+ your rental agreement copy (signed, I hope)
+ a sturdy stick
+ some yellow thread or cord
+ a yellow candle

The Spell
On a full moon, wrap the agreement around one end of the stick and tie it on with the yellow thread, saying:

Evasive, persuasive, now you are here.
Now bound to this rod,
now this you shall hear.
Servitor audiat!
You are this and this is that!

Name the rod after your landlord and yell at it. Call it a &!%!
and a ∂##! and tell him or her exactly what needs fixing.
Then, light the candle saying:

Come with the light, come when it's right.
Do as I say, do it today!

Rap the rod on the floor, walls, ceiling, and anything
that needs fixing. Be severe but don't break anything.
Stop and touch the floor, saying:

SERVITOR AUDIAT,
YOU ARE THIS AND THIS IS THAT.
I PAY THEE—TAKE CARE OF ME!
AS I WILL SO MOTE IT BE!

Put out the candle with the rod. Keep the rod around, and light the candle and repeat steps two and three as needed. When you move out of the apartment, burn the agreement—but leave the rod and a copy of this ritual in a semihidden place for the next tenant!

Man Trouble Spell

Want to wash that man right out of your hair?
Well, here's how.

You Will Need
+ a black candle
+ a match
+ scissors
+ a picture of you and the man

THE SPELL

Light the candle. Take the scissors and cut
the picture of the two of you right down the middle.
Think of how much better your life will be without
him around, and burn his half of the
picture using the fire from the candle. Laugh a lot,
like a cat. Take a shower and let the candle burn out.
It is best to perform this spell
on the dark side of the moon.

A Hex on People Who Give You Bad Directions

If you've asked someone for directions and you get
terminally lost, it was probably not intentional. If it
happens a few times, however, or you know that the person
giving directions was messing with you, use this one
on her and she'll think twice before sending
another poor fool off into the ozone.

You Will Need
+ a piece of map—one she touched is best
+ a black pen

THE SPELL

At a crossroads at night, at the height of anger, take the
map piece in your left hand and the pen in the other
(reversed if you are left-handed). Be very near a
storm sewer grate. Then face toward each of the
four streets in turn, saying:

HERE, THERE, EARTH TO AIR.
WITHOUT A CARE, WHO KNOWS WHERE?

Spin around counterclockwise a number of times until
you are dizzy, thinking of the perpetrator, saying:

TOSSED AND TURNED,
YOUR MIND IS CHURNED.

Stop suddenly, dizzy, then draw a confused
spiral on the map chaotically.
Visualize the direction-giver very lost, saying:

MAY YOU WANDER LOST AND DIZZY,
I SEND YOU OFF IN A CHAOS TIZZY.
BACK TO YOU, BACK TO YOU
OFF YOU GO,
THIS NOW IS TRUE!

Toss the piece of map down into the sewer and picture
the guilty one wandering off. Laugh and leave.

THE HEX OF THE EVIL EYE

If you need to get rid of a nasty dog or someone who is
eyeing you, flash him this one. This works well, but be
careful—you don't want to throw the evil eye at just anyone!

YOU WILL NEED
+ a piece of jewelry that is sacred to you
(a bloodstone or hematite is good)

THE SPELL
Lock your eyes and give your fierce look to someone that
you want to curse. Imagine your gaze burning into their
third eye. Hold the piece of jewelry in your left hand while
you are staring—feel the jewelry protecting you.
Think evil thoughts.

HEX TO GET A SUPPORT CHECK FROM A DEADBEAT

So he stiffed you and the offspring again?
Try this . . . and then the court.

YOU WILL NEED
+ a photo of the deadbeat
+ scissors
+ a blank personal check
+ a pen
+ a candle

THE SPELL

Take the photo of the offending one and cut a slot down
the middle of his body. Take the check and make it out to
yourself, but sign it by the deadbeat. Make it out for the
exact amount you are owed. By candlelight, put the check
behind the photo so just a corner is
showing through the slit and say:

DON'T BE CHEAP!
DON'T BE TIGHT!
(NAME) SEND MY MONEY,
IT'S MY RIGHT!
DONE TODAY,
SENT TONIGHT,
DO IT NOW,
GET IT RIGHT!

Pull the check through the slot, while saying:

Here it comes,
Here it comes
In my pocket,
In my hand
Now!

Once you've pulled the check through the photo, grab it tight. Then jump for joy and toss the check in the air. Visualize it coming to you. Repeat this hex until you get the check. If the next one is late, do it again!

Hex Against Burglars and Muggers

If your car, house, or person is ripped-off, and there is little
hope of getting back what was lost, there is always revenge.
Make the thieves sorry they ever saw your stuff.

You Will Need
+ some black cloth
+ a foul substance (up to you)
+ black thread

The Spell

Take the piece of black cloth and rub where you know
the thief has touched or stepped, saying:

I CATCH YOU,
I'VE GOT YOU
EVIL THIEF.
I BIND YOU,
I HOLD YOU,
YOU'LL HAVE NO RELIEF!

Carefully scoop the foul stuff into the cloth
without touching it. Then say:

AS YOU VIOLATED ME,
I VIOLATE YOU.
MY PEACE YOU DID SLAY,
I DO THIS TO YOU.
YOUR DIRT IN MY LIFE,
I DUMP ON YOUR HEAD!

MAY YOU NEVER FORGET
UNTIL YOU ARE DEAD!

Bind up the cloth with the thread into a little bag and
throw it in a dumpster. As you throw it away, chant:

THE THINGS YOU TOOK ARE ASHES AND RUST.
ALL THAT YOU TOUCH WILL NOW TURN TO DUST.
SO LONG AS YOU STEAL, YOUR LIFE WILL BE SH⁺T.
I TOSS YOU AWAY AND INTO THE PIT!
BYE, BYE!

"I'm Not a Bimbo!" Spell

Just because you are ravishing, alluring, and playful doesn't mean you aren't bright, witty, and intelligent. In fact, if you are a woman, you probably possess all of these qualities and more! This spell will stop someone from being condescending to you.

You Will Need

+ a dark red candle
+ a match
+ a garnet or ruby

The Spell

Before you start your day, light the candle, chanting:

FIRE STONE,
FIRE MY OWN.
FIRE BURN,
NEVER TURN.
LET ALL SEE
YOU ARE WITH ME,
IGNIS!

Wear the stone to work. When someone is being
condescending or ignoring you, rub the stone,
look at him, and whisper:

I AM FIRE, SEE ME BURN!
YOUR BACK TO ME NEVER TURN!
STEP ON ME AND YOU WILL YELL,
MESS WITH ME, YOU MESS WITH HELL!
IGNIS!

Then smile your best and brightest smile.

About the Author

Sophia is a professional psychic and spiritual teacher with more than twenty years of experience, both in the U.S. and abroad. Part Native American, she was taught how to tap her psychic powers by her grandparents when she was a child. From the age of three, she learned psychic reading, card reading, coffee-ground reading, astrology, and other forms of divination. She is also a professional photographer. Her previous book, *Fortunetelling With Playing Cards*, was published in 1996. *The Sophia Deck of Fortunetelling Cards* will be published in 1997.